STARS: Steps to Achieving Real-life Skills

Respecting Others

Dear Student:

This workbook is part of a program to help you learn some real-life skills. You may already have some of these skills, and the information may just be a reminder or a review. If the information is new to you, then it is possible for you to learn skills and strategies that can help you for the rest of your life.

If you are unable to complete any section, leave it blank and come back to it later. If you are still unsure, ask your parent or guardian to assist you. If this is not possible, ask the person who gave you the workbook. On the next page there is a glossary of words that are used in the workbook. Read this before you begin.

Please remember to have your parent or guardian fill out the last page.

Thank you for your cooperation.

Name of Student: _____

Adviser: _____

Assignment Date: _____

Completion Date: _____

Glossary

Assertive—able to stand up for one's rights and, at the same time, respect the rights of others

Body Language—the way in which a person stands, sits, or moves and how these gestures and movements communicate what the person is thinking or feeling to others

Concentration—the ability to focus or pay attention

Consequence—the result of an action, an event, or your behavior

Discrimination—treating people differently or unfairly because of race, color, sex, or other differences

Empathy—the ability to understand or feel the thoughts or feelings of others

Prejudice—an opinion that may be based on partial information and can be harmful to others

Race—a section of humankind that shares a certain heritage and characteristics

Racist—a person who believes that people's abilities are determined by their race

Relaxation Technique—a skill or activity that you can use to calm yourself

Rumor—talk or opinions that are started by an unknown person and are usually not accurate

Technique—a method or way of doing something

Respecting Others

People who respect others see others as unique human beings with many differences. Respectful people are generally good listeners. People who are respectful also have empathy, they are tolerant of others, they can be trusted, and they communicate well. If you respect the rights of others, you will get along better with people. **Using a dictionary, look up the following words, which will be used in this unit.**

Expression _____

Empathy _____

Stereotype _____

Discrimination _____

Tolerance _____

Prejudice _____

Respect _____

Integrity _____

Neutral _____

Now mix up the beginning letters to all the words to spell another word. Here are the letters: E, E, S, D, T, P, R, I, N.

What is the mystery word? _____

Rights and Expectations

Respecting others means that you live up to basic expectations from people in your life such as parents and teachers. Respecting others also means that you recognize and appreciate the basic rights of each person. If you are aware of these personal rights and of the expectations of the people who have taught you right from wrong, you will be able to recognize when you need to change in order to be more respectful.

What rights do you have? *e.g., the right to speak*

1._____

2._____

3._____

What rights do others have? *e.g., the right to be treated with respect*

1._____

2._____

3._____

What do people at school expect from you? *e.g., to arrive on time with supplies*

1._____

2._____

3._____

What do parents/guardians expect from you? *e.g., to tell the truth*

1._____

2._____

3._____

Everyone makes mistakes. Sometimes we do things that aren't respectful to ourselves or others. Think about the last mistake you made that was either against your family's expectations or against the school rules.

Could you have done something worse?

☐ Yes   ☐ No

What would be worse?_____

_____

Did you do the worst thing?

☐ Yes   ☐ No

Are you willing to try to do better?

☐ Yes   ☐ No

How could you do better?

_____

_____

Remember: You are not the only one who has ever made a mistake. It's all right to make a mistake. The most important thing is to fix it. What kind of person do you want to be? What do you believe?

Respect Yourself First

It's hard for others to respect you, if you don't respect yourself. Some signs that show that people don't respect themselves are

1. Not looking after their health.

2. Constantly getting themselves in trouble.

3. Putting down other people.

4. Saying hurtful things about themselves.

How do you think others see you?

If you suddenly had to move away, what would be three comments people would say about you?

Fill in the card below with the comments.

Good Luck!

1. _____
   _____
   _____

2. _____
   _____
   _____

3. _____
   _____
   _____

What Kind of Person Do You Want to Be?

What three things do you want people to remember about you?

1. _____

2. _____

3. _____

Would you say that you're currently acting in a way that will make you the kind of person you want to be in the future?

☐ Yes   ☐ No

Explain why or why not.

_____

_____

_____

_____

_____

_____

The Respect Report

How respectful are you? Do you accept people who are different from you? Do you make fun of people just to go along with your friends? Do you treat others the way you want to be treated? **Take the following quiz and see how you score. Circle the letter beside the answer that *best* describes what you would do in the stated situation.**

1. *You are with a group of friends and you pass someone who is of a different race. Your friend says something racist.*

   a) You agree with her and laugh out loud.

   b) You make another racist joke and everyone laughs.

   c) You don't laugh and tell your friend not to tell racist jokes.

2. *A person in your class is overweight and a lot of people tease him.*

   a) You whisper something mean to a friend and you both laugh because you think overweight people should do something about themselves.

   b) You go along with everyone and call him rude names behind his back.

   c) You keep your thoughts to yourself because you believe it's what's inside someone that matters.

3. *A student is walking down the hall in school and trips over her feet. Her books go flying and she lands on her backside.*

   a) You pick up her books and help her up.

   b) You giggle to yourself and keep walking.

   c) You laugh and call her a "loser."

4. *You're playing a game in gym class, and a student on your team can't play very well.*

   a) You tell him to try harder if he wants to be on your team.

   b) You say out loud, "We don't want a loser—go to the other team."

   c) You encourage him and tell him he's doing just fine.

5. *If you were new to a school, how would you pick friends?*

   a) Always look for people who look and/or act just like you.

   b) Pick people who are popular and have money.

   c) Pick friends who respect you and who want to have you as a friend.

6. *A girl at school only has a few, worn-out outfits and people laugh at her. You know that her parents don't have a lot of money.*

   a) You laugh along with everyone because she could always get clothes from the lost and found box.

   b) You ignore her because you don't want to get caught talking to her.

   c) You tell people to stop bugging her because she deserves respect.

7. *During a test you look up to think and you accidentally look towards another student's paper. The teacher accuses you of cheating.*

   a) You yell back at the teacher and tell him you're sick of him blaming you for everything.

   b) You try to explain politely that you weren't cheating and the teacher is making a mistake.

   c) You give the teacher a mean look. You don't say anything because it's no use—teachers never listen.

8. *A person in school who has to permanently use crutches is having trouble carrying her bag and getting up the stairs.*

   a) You ignore her because it's her problem, not yours.

   b) You laugh because it's so funny, and you don't know what else to do.

   c) You offer to carry her bag and walk with her.

9. *You and your friends are talking in class. The teacher comes in but you don't notice. The teacher asks everyone to be quiet, but you don't hear. You get sent out because you kept talking.*

   a) You leave the room and use the time to think about how to apologize and explain the situation.

   b) You walk out, slam the door, and say it wasn't your fault.

   c) You leave the room and think this teacher is always picking on you, but you will get her back next class.

10. *You are outside playing soccer, and someone on the other team kicks the ball and hits you in the head. It hurts, but you're not injured.*

    a) You leave the game and yell at the person because he should have been more careful.

    b) You go after the kid who hit you because he probably meant to hurt you.

    c) You forgive him because you know that accidents happen during games.

SCORING: Add up your points and match your score to the comments below.

				Your Score
1	A=5	B=10	C=10	_____
2	A=10	B=5	C=0	_____
3	A=0	B=5	C=10	_____
4	A=5	B=10	C=0	_____
5	A=5	B=10	C=0	_____
6	A=10	B=5	C=0	_____
7	A=10	B=0	C=5	_____
8	A=5	B=10	C=0	_____
9	A=0	B=10	C=5	_____
10	A=5	B=10	C=0	_____
			Total:	_____

20 and Under. Very respectful; caring and understanding; open-minded

30–69. Respectful of others; a leader in many situations; generally stick up for yourself and others

70–79. Respectful at times; go along with others; worried about making decisions

80–100. Feel like others pick on you; get angry easily; need to work on understanding others and giving people a chance

How Well Do You Listen?

Listening to others is respectful. Learning to listen to others is a skill. There are a few helpful tips to remember if you want to let others know that you are listening when they are speaking. To help you remember, think of it as a **FOLDER** of information to keep in the back of your mind. Each letter in the word **FOLDER** stands for a listening tip.

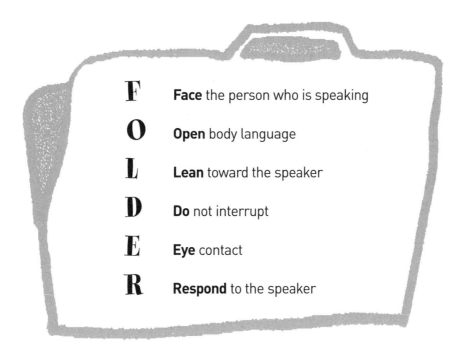

F **Face** the person who is speaking

O **Open** body language

L **Lean** toward the speaker

D **Do** not interrupt

E **Eye** contact

R **Respond** to the speaker

F—It is very important to look at the speaker and to sit opposite him or her whenever possible. If it isn't possible to sit across from him or her, turn your head so that you are facing the speaker.

O—Having open body language means that you look eager to hear what the speaker is saying. This means that you don't cross your legs or arms, and that you sit up straight. When your body is open, it looks like you are interested in what the speaker is saying.

L—Leaning slightly forward towards the speaker is another helpful tip. This again shows that you are interested in what the person is saying. Try not to slouch back in the chair.

D—Do not interrupt. Interrupting stops the speaker and it may cause the speaker to forget what he or she was going to say. Wait for a natural pause in the sentence or until the speaker finishes. Respond to what the speaker said and let him or her know that you understood.

E—Keep your eyes on the speaker at all times. If you look away, the speaker will notice and it will appear that you aren't listening.

R—Respond to the speaker by either telling the speaker what you heard or by clarifying what was said. If you are uncertain about anything that was said, ask a question to ensure that you do understand.

Distractions

Good listeners are not easily distracted. A respectful person tries his or her best not to be distracted when others are talking. A distraction might be something that catches your eye or a sound you hear in the distance. Knowing what distracts you may help you learn to be a more respectful listener.

What distracts you? **List four things that you may find distracting.**

1._____

2._____

3._____

4._____

If you have any trouble with the previous question, wait until you talk to someone and then take note of the times that you might be distracted. During a lesson at school, there may be several distractions at one time. How about in a busy mall or another place where there are lots of people?

In the space below, draw a picture of one of your distractions.

Empathy

Respectful people are able to appreciate and show compassion for others. This is called having empathy. People who have empathy are also able to understand how others must feel in a situation. They are able to feel as if they were in the other person's shoes. Recognizing how others feel and responding to them with empathy shows kindness and respect. **For the following scenarios, write down how you would feel if you were in another person's shoes.**

Situation 1

Nico and Marcello are two of the biggest kids in the class. Both of the boys have a history of being violent and they have both been suspended from school on numerous occasions. One morning they surround Liu and demand that he empty his pockets. When they see that he has a watch and a $10 bill, they quickly grab them and push him into a desk.

Put yourself in Liu's shoes. How would you feel? _____

_____

_____

Situation 2

Haley is a new girl to grade eight and she doesn't know anyone in the entire school. Lana, who is one of the toughest girls in eighth grade, has decided that no one should hang out with Haley because she is a minority. Lana says that if anyone is nice to Haley, Lana will beat that person up. Lana has been calling Haley racist names.

Put yourself into Haley's shoes. How would you feel if you were Haley? _____

_____

_____

Does Haley deserve this treatment? _____

_____

What should be done about Lana? _____

_____

Situation 3

Davis was in a car accident a year ago and suffered a head injury. When Davis tries to answer a question in class he stutters because he is still recovering. The class clown, Colin, always imitates Davis and this makes the class laugh.

Put yourself into Davis's shoes. How would you feel if you were Davis?_____

_____

_____

_____

Does Davis deserve to be made fun of? Explain._____

_____

_____

_____

Situation 4

When Natalya comes home from school, her mom is drunk. Her mom starts to yell at Natalya and call her names. She tells Natalya to change her outfit because she looks like a tramp. This morning Natalya's mom told her she looked nice in the same clothes. Natalya doesn't say anything back because she is scared. This makes her mom angrier, and Natalya's mom throws her glass at her and cuts Natalya's arm.

Put yourself into Natalya's shoes. How would you feel if you were Natalya? _____

_____

_____

_____

Does Natalya deserve to feel like this? Explain. _____

_____

_____

_____

Respectful Roles

In different situations we often have different roles. Some of our roles might be more appropriate in one setting than in others. For example, with your friends you might be a leader and a joker, but with a grandparent, this might not be a respectful role to choose. If you are aware of what roles you have in different situations, you might be able to recognize why you are acting differently and choose a more respectful role.

What are your roles? List as many as you can think of.

_____

_____

_____

_____

_____

_____

What role do you play at home?

_____

How do you feel when you play this role?

_____

What role do you play with your friends?

_____

How do you feel when you play this role?

_____

What role do you play in your favorite class?

_____

How do you feel when you play this role?

_____

What role do you play in your least favorite class?

_____

How do you feel when you play this role?

_____

If you find yourself acting disrespectfully, first ask yourself how you feel and what role you are playing. Is this the best role for the situation? Can you think of a role that would be more respectful?

Hearing What Others Say

Many times not hearing what people really say or misunderstanding what they say causes problems. Rumors may be spread or lies may be started. People may get hurt because the truth isn't known to others. Communicating is not talking **AT** someone—it is talking **WITH** that person. Paraphrasing is used to respond to what another person has said. Try to repeat what you heard the person say to you in only one or two sentences. Doing this tells the person that you listened to and understood what they said. Some ways to begin a paraphrase are the following:

It sounds like . . .

I heard you say . . .

It seems like . . .

I sense that you . . .

For example:

Suppose that your friend tells you that her locker has been broken into, and all her things have been stolen. She has tears in her eyes, and she's worried because she doesn't have money to buy more supplies until the end of the month.

An example of how you would paraphrase what she said is, *"You sound like you're really upset about your locker and worried about having to replace everything."*

Imagine that a very close friend says the following statements to you. **Try paraphrasing what is written in the following situations.**

Example 1

I'm so mad I could scream. I can't believe that this has happened again. Every single time I pass by that kid, he trips me and pushes me into someone. I'm going to lose it if he keeps this up.

Your paraphrase: _____

_____

_____

_____

_____

Example 2

My mom and dad said I can go! I get to go to camp for two weeks without my sister. I finally get to do something on my own without her tagging along. I can't wait to leave.

Your paraphrase: _____

_____

_____

_____

_____

Example 3

"I'm such a loser. I'm never going to high school. I can't seem to pass even one stupid test. I hate school. I want to quit."

Your paraphrase: _____

_____

_____

_____

_____

Example 4

In one way I really do want to move because I get to go to a totally different place. It's just that I'm going to miss everyone so much.

Your paraphrase: _____

_____

_____

_____

_____

Try paraphrasing a real conversation. Ask someone at home or school about what happened today. What was good or bad? See if you can let them speak and then follow with a short paraphrase of what you heard them say. **Write the person's own account of their day and then write your paraphrase below it.**

Their story: _____

_____

_____

_____

_____

Your paraphrase: _____

_____

_____

_____

_____

_____

So You're Angry—What Are You Going to Do About It?

Being respectful requires that you control your anger and deal with it positively. The following ideas are called control techniques. To help you remember the techniques, remember the words **ICE CREAM.**

I   Imagine somewhere calm

C   Count backwards

E   Exercise

C   Consequence acceptance

R   Relaxation techniques

E   Either solve it…or leave it

A   Assert yourself

M   Music

Imagine Somewhere Calm

Thinking about a nice place can have a pleasant effect on your body. The best part about this is it can be anywhere you want. You might even imagine being somewhere out of this world.

Count Backwards

Counting backwards from twenty slowly can help you get control of yourself. It gives you time to STOP…THINK…THEN ACT. This technique gives you time to think about the best way to act.

Exercise

Exercise like walking, running, skating, or biking can do wonders for your body. Exercise will not only help you calm down if you are already angry, but also it will help prevent you from feeling angry in the first place. When your body is healthy, your mind is healthy. A lot of people feel sad or irritable when they don't exercise daily. Any exercise is better than no exercise. Find a routine that works for you.

Consequence Acceptance

Sometimes we make mistakes and there is a logical consequence that follows. In some circumstances, accepting the consequences without becoming discouraged is the best reaction. If you made a mistake, fix it. For example, if you insult someone, apologize.

Relaxation Techniques

Learning to relax is a skill that many people could use. Some common techniques are: taking deep breaths, tensing and then relaxing the different parts of your body, or visualization (imagining yourself in a happy or calm place). Athletes often use this technique before an event to help them relax and concentrate.

Either Solve It...or Leave It

Sometimes, though, the timing just isn't right for problem solving and it might be a better idea to walk away from the situation for a while and come back to it later when you are feeling more ready.

Assert Yourself

There are several methods for being assertive. One of the most common methods is to use an "I" message. An "I" message is an assertive technique used to respond to someone who is trying to provoke you. Here is the formula:

> *When you...*
>
> *I feel...*
>
> *because...*
>
> *I need...*

Here is how it might sound:

> *When you* take my book,
>
> *I feel* mad
>
> *because* I have to do my work.
>
> *I need* you to give it back.

Here is another example:

> *When you* call me names,
>
> *I feel* hurt
>
> *because* it embarrasses me.
>
> *I need* you to stop insulting me.

1. *Your friend borrowed your hat without asking and lost it.*

When you _____

I feel _____

because _____

I need _____

2. *A person in your class always demands that you give him or her your work and you keep getting zeros for not having any work.*

When you _____

I feel _____

because _____

I need _____

3. *A person you were friends with is making up stories about you and spreading them around the school.*

When you _____

I feel _____

because _____

I need _____

It's okay to let people know that they have hurt your feelings or made you angry. If someone insults you, try asking them:

Was that supposed to hurt my feelings?
If they say "yes," say, *"Well, it did."*
If they say "no," say, *"Well, it did."*
Either way you have an answer.

Music

The last technique for controlling your anger is to use music. Music can help to change your mood. Lively music might make you feel energetic; slower music, on the other hand, might help you calm down. Music can also help to distract some negative feelings and help you put yourself somewhere else that might be more positive.

What song would you listen to if you wanted to cool off?

_____

by _____

What song would you listen to if you wanted to get energy, or put yourself in a good mood?

_____

by _____

What song would you listen to if you were really sad?

_____

by _____

What song would you listen to if you were extremely happy?

_____

by _____

Use your imagination to create your own verse to a song:

_____

_____

_____

_____

_____

Respecting Differences

One thing that all respectful people do is appreciate differences. Being respectful means that you accept each person's uniqueness and individuality. We are all different and our differences should be celebrated, not discriminated against.

List five ways that all people are alike:

1._____

2._____

3._____

4._____

5._____

List five ways that people are different:

1._____

2._____

3._____

4._____

5._____

What is one quality you have that makes you different from other people?

_____

20

Respecting Differences: An Interview

Discrimination separates people and encourages prejudiced thinking. Learning about discrimination and thinking about the effects of discrimination makes it easier to do something about it. Respecting each person as an important and worthy individual will ensure that everyone feels respected.

Ask someone you know (a parent, teacher, family member, etc.) to tell you about an example of discrimination in our society. In your own words, write down the example below.

_____

_____

If you could magically solve this problem, what would you do?

_____

_____

Now think of a time when you may have been discriminated against. Briefly explain the situation.

_____

_____

At the time, how did you feel about it?

_____

What did you do about it?

_____

_____

If you answered "nothing" to the question above, explain why.

_____

_____

Why would people discriminate against others or be prejudiced?

_____

_____

Friendship

Think about what kind of friend you are or have been. What kind of friend would you like to be? Do your friendships change frequently or do they last a long time? Have you had friendships that ended poorly? People who make friends easily and get along with a variety of people usually have friendships that last a long time. **They are able to work through problems in their friendships by being respectful, courteous, and thoughtful.**

1. How have your friendships changed over the past year or two?_____

_____

2. What do you value in your best friend(s)? _____

_____

3. What do your friends value in you? _____

_____

4. Is it easy for you to make friends?   ☐ Yes   ☐ No

   If not, what seems to make it difficult? _____

   _____

5. Is it easy for you to keep friendships going?   ☐ Yes   ☐ No

   If not, what seems to cause problems?_____

   _____

6. Do you have friends of different ages?   ☐ Yes   ☐ No

7. What are some things you and your friends have in common? _____

_____

8. What are some things you and your friends don't have in common? _____

_____

9. What makes friendships different for people your age than for people a few years younger than you?

_____

_____

10. What do you think makes adult friendships different from friendships at your age?

_____

_____

11. Do you have some friends your parents don't approve of? ☐ Yes ☐ No

If so, what kinds of problems does that cause for you? _____

_____

12. What have you learned through friendships? _____

_____

13. Have you ever lost a friend because one of you moved away? ☐ Yes ☐ No

If you have, was it difficult to adjust to that loss? ☐ Yes ☐ No

14. Have you ever felt rejected by a friend? ☐ Yes ☐ No

If you have, how did you help yourself handle the rejection? _____

_____

Do you still think about it? ☐ Yes ☐ No

15. Do you quickly develop close friendships, or are you slow to become involved in a close friendship? _____

_____

16. What advice would you give to someone who has difficulty making friends?

_____

_____

Being a Good Friend

Everyone has his or her own definition of a friend. Most people look for specific characteristics in their friends. Sometimes people are friends, and then they decide that they no longer want to be friends. People change and may become closer or grow apart. Most people like to be accepted by their peers. People usually belong to a group that they feel comfortable with. Most people agree that there are some common characteristics that they find necessary to create a solid friendship.

List three qualities that are important for you when choosing a friend.

1._____

2._____

3._____

List three things friends would say to each other.

1._____

2._____

3._____

List three things friends would not say to each other.

1._____

2._____

3._____

Remember:

To have a friend, you need to be one!

Close Ties

Below are some qualities that are important in choosing friends. When people talk about their friends, they say that they have close ties. Using the phrase **CLOSE TIES** can help you remember the friendship qualities.

C **Communicate** (talk or write to each other)

L **Listen** (make an effort to pay attention to your friends)

O **Optimism** (focus on the positive and be hopeful)

S **Share and support** (be there when they need you)

E **Enthusiasm** (be active and show you are interested in them)

T **Trust** (be reliable and responsible)

I **Involve yourself** (participate in activities you both enjoy)

E **Equality** (treat all people as equals)

S **Solve problems** (work through conflict and troubles)

Design a billboard sign to encourage younger kids to follow the CLOSE TIES qualities. You may include one or several qualities to show on the sign.

What are some ways to meet new people or make friends?

List the ways you can think of to meet new people or make friends.

_____   _____

_____   _____

_____   _____

_____

Unfortunately, not all friends are worth keeping. Sometimes people we think are our friends turn out to be using us. Sometimes they end up being very different from how we expected them to be.

Some examples of when a friend is not being a friend are:

1. When a friend pressures you into stealing something from a store for him or her.

2. When a friend tells you he or she is keeping what you say to himself or herself and then tells a bunch of other people what you said to embarrass you.

3. When a friend lies to you or makes fun of you behind your back.

List three more examples of when a friend may not be worth keeping.

1._____

2._____

3._____

Sometimes a friend may need help, and you're the only one who can help him or her. If a friend tells you a secret that puts him or her in personal danger, or you believe that your friend's personal safety or the safety of others is in danger, then you need to tell an adult about it so that your friend is safe.

26

Respecting the Trust of Others

A person who can be relied on or trusted makes a terrific friend. Someone that others can depend on to share information with or to follow through on an agreement earns respect from others. People who spread rumors or share private information usually end up hurting someone and losing the respect of others. How trustworthy are you? What could you do to be more trustworthy? **Check the answer that best describes you.**

1. Do you keep private information (secrets) to yourself?

   ☐ never   ☐ sometimes   ☐ always

2. Do you spread rumors?

   ☐ never   ☐ sometimes   ☐ always

3. Have you ever had a rumor spread about you?

   ☐ Yes   ☐ No

4. Has someone ever not kept a secret that you told him or her?

   ☐ Yes   ☐ No

5. Check the feelings you would have if someone spread a very mean rumor about you at school.

   ☐ angry   ☐ sad   ☐ hurt   ☐ embarrassed
   ☐ disappointed   ☐ annoyed   ☐ mad

6. Imagine this situation:

   You tell a friend that you like someone at school. Your friend tells someone else and he or she tells five more people. Soon the whole class knows that you like the person. Check how you might be feeling.

   ☐ angry   ☐ frustrated   ☐ betrayed   ☐ enraged
   ☐ embarrassed   ☐ humiliated   ☐ annoyed   ☐ disappointed   ☐ upset

7. How can you stop someone from telling a secret? _____

_____

8. What would make someone spread a rumor or tell a secret? _____

_____

9. If you accidentally let a secret out, what three things could you do to make the situation better?

1. _____

2. _____

3. _____

If you or someone you know is in danger...

For example:

Someone is hurting him or her

The person may hurt himself or herself

The person may hurt someone else

It's okay to tell someone you trust who can help...

Such as:

A teacher

A counselor

A parent or other adult

The Five Questions

1. false is rumor this a?

_____

2. secret someone spread it to your if would was it you want ?

_____

3. sorry you it say after you will be ?

_____

4. hurt help or tell to it will ?

_____

5. others does respect of the it rights ?

_____

If you are ever unsure about what to do or how to react to a particular situation, ask yourself these five questions. Use them to help you make the best choice.

Journal Writing–Reflecting

Take a moment to think about the work you have done in this workbook. **Jot down some words about how you felt working on this workbook.** From there, use a sentence starter to write about what you have accomplished. Pick the sentence starter that you like and write a paragraph about anything you want. This is a chance for you to be creative and to write something for yourself. Use the space below and a separate sheet if necessary.

If you are better with pictures, feel free to draw a picture.

Sentence Starters

A friend...

Accepting others is important because...

Being a good friend is...

I like to hang out with people who...

_____

_____

_____

_____

_____

_____

_____

Respecting Others

Parents/Guardians

It would be helpful if you could review and comment on the work that your child has done in this workbook. We encourage students to work with their parents on certain sections and we thank you for your cooperation. We hope that your child has had a chance to examine their behavior and to plan positively for the future. This unit has exposed students to a lot of information which we hope could be reviewed at home. We greatly appreciate your partnership in this project.

Comments: _____

_____

_____

_____

_____

_____

_____

Please feel free to contact the student's advisor or the person who assigned this workbook if you have any other questions or concerns.

Students

Now that you have completed the workbook, we urge you to provide some comments. Please comment on anything positive, e.g. "What did you like about it?" Also comment on what you did not like. If you have any suggestions, we would also like to hear them. **Congratulations for all your hard work!**

Comments: _____

_____

_____

_____

_____

_____

_____